OLYMPICS '96

OLYMPIC HISTORY

The Ancient Olympics

From their earliest beginnings the Olympic Games have been a celebration of sporting effort and achievement. Arising out of the legendary contests between the Greek gods over 3,000 years ago, the first Olympics were religious as well as sporting occasions. The first recorded Olympic Games took place at Olympia in Greece in 776BC.

In Roman times however, the Olympics were affected by corrupt judges and 'professional' competitors specially hired to represent certain countries. Eventually, in AD393, Emperor Theodosius I banned the Games and the Ancient Olympics came to an end.

Greek statue of the discus thrower, Discobolos

The Modern Olympics

Baron Pierre de Coubertin – founder of the modern Olympics

The idea of reviving the Olympic Games became a reality when Baron Pierre de Coubertin announced his plan to relaunch the Games in 1892.

The first modern Games took place in Athens, Greece in 1896. Most of the competitors were Greek, with many of the foreign competitors only entering because they happened to be in Greece on holiday or business at the time!

In the Olympics of today, great emphasis is placed on being the best, but even greater importance is attached to trying your best. For many sportsmen and sportswomen, the pinnacle of their sporting life is just to appear at the Olympic Games – the greatest sporting event in the world.

ATLANTA '96
20 July to 4 August

Years of preparation and planning went into Atlanta's bid to stage the Olympic Games in 1996. With five other strong bids from Athens, Belgrade, Manchester, Melbourne and Toronto, the Americans were not favourites to hold the Centennial Games. Indeed, many people believed that Athens was the most likely venue to commemorate

'WHATIZIT' the official mascot of the 1996 Olympic Games

100 years of the modern Olympics. So it was a welcome surprise for Atlanta to be awarded the 1996 Games in September 1990.

Most of the events at the Atlanta Games will be held at two venues – the Olympic Ring in the centre of the city and the Olympic Park at Stone Mountain, 27 kilometres outside Atlanta.

The Olympic Ring is an imaginary circle with a radius of 2.5 kilometres containing the Olympic Stadium, the Olympic Family Hotel, the Olympic Village and the Olympic Center.

The yachting events take place at the Yachting Marina at Savannah on the Georgia coast.

The Olympic stadium – location for the opening and closing ceremonies; track and field events and the finals of the football at Atlanta '96

* Atlanta is the state capital of Georgia in the southeast of the United States. The city has a population of about three million.

* Seven and a half million tickets will be sold for events in the 1996 Olympic Games.

* The Olympic Village will be host to around 15,500 athletes and officials.

OLYMPIC SPORTS FOR '96

Archery

Archery is probably one of the oldest of all sports in the world and is thought to have become an organised sport in the 3rd century AD. It was first included in the modern Games in 1900.

Individual events

In the individual events each competitor fires 36 arrows at each of four targets. In the men's event, the targets are placed at 90, 70, 50 and 30 metres. For women the distances are 70, 60, 50 and 30 metres. The target is divided into ten rings, with the inner ring worth 10 points and the outer ring worth 1 point. The 32 archers with the best scores progress to the knockout stage in which they fire 12 arrows from a distance of 70 metres. The medals are awarded to the three highest scorers.

Team events

Nations for the team events are selected on the basis of scores achieved in the individual events. Only the 16 top-scoring teams go on to an elimination round where each team member fires nine arrows at a target 70 metres distant. Medal positions are awarded to the three highest scoring teams.

Archery scoring

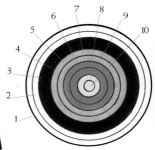

Archery targets have ten zones depicted in five different colours. Each colour has an inner and outer ring scoring differently

Natalia Valeeva (EUN) bronze medallist in the individual event – Barcelona, 1992

Sebastien Flute (France) winning gold in the individual event at the Olympics, 1992

Event	1992 winner	1996 winner
Women's		
Individual	Y-J. Cho (S. Korea)	....
Team	S. Korea	....
Men's		
Individual	S. Flute (France)	....
Team	Spain	....

DID YOU KNOW?
• Charlotte Dod (Great Britain), silver medallist in the individual archery events in 1908, also won the British Ladies' Golf title, represented England at hockey and was Wimbledon Singles Champion five times.

VENUE: ARCHERY FIELD, OLYMPIC PARK AT STONE MOUNTAIN

Athletics

Athletics track and field events have been included in the modern Games since they began in 1896. The Olympic stadium will host all the 1996 athletics events, although the walks and the marathons take place on the road and only finish in the stadium. Track and field athletics always provide the main focal point of the Games.

Track events

Track races

An Olympic running track, which is oval in shape, is 400 metres per lap and is divided into eight lanes.

The 100 metre sprint is run on the straight but the 200 metre and 400 metre sprints have 'staggered' starting points to equalise the distance to be run. Competitors must stay in their lanes in all sprint races.

The 800 metres race also has a 'staggered' start but runners may break lanes at the end of the first lap of the track. Longer races are not run in lanes.

The start of the 100 metres final in 1896

The 1,500 metres is three and three-quarter laps, the women's 3,000 metres is seven and a half laps, the men's 5,000 metres is twelve and a half laps and the 10,000 metres races are 25 laps of the track.

Linford Christie (Great Britain) wins the 100 metres final – Olympic Games, 1992

DID YOU KNOW?

• One of the greatest long distance runners of all time was Emil Zatopek (Czechoslovakia). Following his 10,000 metres gold medal win at the 1948 Olympics, he not only won the gold in the 5,000 metres at the 1952 Games in Helsinki, but also won the 10,000 metres and the marathon.

William Tanui (Kenya), the 1992
800 metres Olympic champion

Relays

In relay teams, there are four athletes. Each athlete runs a 'leg' of the race and then passes a baton on to the next runner. There are two relay events for men and women – the 4 x 100 metres (one lap of the track in total) and the 4 x 400 metres (four laps of the track). Relay races are traditionally the last event and bring the Games to an end.

Hurdles and steeplechase

There are ten hurdles, or 'flights', in each of the four Olympic hurdle events. The heights of these hurdles vary considerably – 1.06 metres in the men's 110 metres event, 0.91 metres in the men's 400 metres event, 0.84 metres in the women's 100 metres event and 0.76 metres in the women's 400 metres event.

The men's 3,000 metre steeplechase event has 28 hurdles 0.91 metres high and seven water jumps 3.65 metres long with a maximum depth of 0.69 metres. Hurdles knocked down unintentionally do not result in disqualification, but can make the hurdler slower.

Walks

In walking races, athletes must keep at least one foot in contact with the ground at all times and must straighten their legs with each step. Olympic walking events take place on the open road but finish on the track in the main Olympic Stadium.

Marathons

A marathon is run over 26 miles, plus a single 385 yard lap of the stadium track. A women's marathon was introduced into the Olympics as recently as 1984. Marathon runners usually encounter physical problems after 17 miles when they hit a tiredness barrier known as the 'wall'.

At the end of each track race the competitor who crosses the finishing line first with his or her torso (not arms, legs or head) is the winner.

Sally Gunnell –
one of Britain's
top gold medallist
winners at
Barcelona, 1992

Women's track events

Event	1992 winner and time	1996 winner and time
100 metres	G. Devers (United States)	....
Winning time:	10.82 seconds	....
Olympic record:	10.54 seconds	New record? Yes / No
200 metres	G. Torrence (United States)	....
Winning time:	21.81 seconds	....
Olympic record:	21.34 seconds	New record? Yes / No
400 metres	M-J. Perec (France)	....
Winning time:	48.83 seconds	....
Olympic record:	48.65 seconds	New record? Yes / No
800 metres	E. Van Langen (Netherlands)	....
Winning time:	1 minute 55.54 seconds	....
Olympic record:	1 minute 53.43 seconds	New record? Yes / No
1,500 metres	H. Boulmerka (Algeria)	....
Winning time:	3 minutes 55.30 seconds	....
Olympic record:	3 minutes 53.96 seconds	New record? Yes / No
3,000 metres	E. Romanova (EUN)	....
Winning time:	8 minutes 46.04 seconds	....
Olympic record:	8 minutes 26.53 seconds	New record? Yes / No
10,000 metres	D. Tulu (Ethiopia)	....
Winning time:	31 minutes 06.02 seconds	....
Olympic record:	31 minutes 05.21 seconds	New record? Yes / No
Marathon	V. Yegorova (EUN)	....
Winning time:	2 hours 32.41 minutes	....
Olympic record:	2 hours 24.52 minutes	New record? Yes / No
10 kilometre walk	Y. Chen (China)	....
Winning time:	44.32 minutes	....
Olympic record:	44.32 minutes	New record? Yes / No
100 metre hurdles	P. Patoulidou (Greece)	....
Winning time:	12.64 seconds	....
Olympic record:	12.38 seconds	New record? Yes / No
400 metre hurdles	S. Gunnell (Great Britain)	....
Winning time:	53.23 seconds	....
Olympic record:	53.17 seconds	New record? Yes / No
4 x 100 metres	United States	....
Winning time:	42.11 seconds	....
Olympic record:	41.60 seconds	New record? Yes / No
4 x 400 metres	EUN	....
Winning time:	3 minutes 20.20 seconds	....
Olympic record:	3 minutes 15.17 seconds	New record? Yes / No

Men's track events		
Event	1992 winner and time	1996 winner and time
100 metres Winning time: Olympic record:	L. Christie (Great Britain) 9.96 seconds 9.92 seconds	.... New record? Yes / No
200 metres Winning time: Olympic record:	M. Marsh (United States) 20.01 seconds 19.75 seconds	.... New record? Yes / No
400 metres Winning time: Olympic record:	Q. Watts (United States) 43.50 seconds 43.50 seconds	.... New record? Yes / No
800 metres Winning time: Olympic record:	W. Tanui (Kenya) 1 minute 43.66 seconds 1 minute 43.00 seconds	.... New record? Yes / No
1,500 metres Winning time: Olympic record:	F. Cacho Ruiz (Spain) 3 minutes 40.12 seconds 3 minutes 32.53 seconds	.... New record? Yes / No
5,000 metres Winning time: Olympic record:	D. Baumann (Germany) 13 minutes 12.52 seconds 13 minutes 05.59 seconds	.... New record? Yes / No
10,000 metres Winning time: Olympic record:	K. Skah (Morocco) 27 minutes 46.70 seconds 27 minutes 21.46 seconds	.... New record? Yes / No
Marathon Winning time: Olympic record:	Y-C. Hwang (S. Korea) 2 hours 13.23 minutes 2 hours 09.21 minutes	.... New record? Yes / No
20 kilometre walk Winning time: Olympic record:	D. Plaza (Spain) 1 hour 21.45 minutes 1 hour 19.57 minutes	.... New record? Yes / No
50 kilometre walk Winning time: Olympic record:	A. Perlov (EUN) 3 hours 50.13 minutes 3 hours 38.29 minutes	.... New record? Yes / No
110 metre hurdles Winning time: Olympic record:	M. McKoy (Canada) 13.12 seconds 12.98 seconds	.... New record? Yes / No
400 metre hurdles Winning time: Olympic record:	K. Young (United States) 46.78 seconds 46.78 seconds	.... New record? Yes / No
3,000 metre steeplechase Winning time: Olympic record:	M. Birir (Kenya) 8 minutes 08.84 seconds 8 minutes 05.51 seconds	.... New record? Yes / No

Event	1992 winner and time	1996 winner and time
4 x 100 metres	United States	....
Winning time:	37.40 seconds	....
Olympic record:	37.40 seconds	New record? Yes / No
4 x 400 metres	United States	....
Winning time:	2 minutes 55.74 seconds	....
Olympic record:	2 minutes 55.74 seconds	New record? Yes / No

Field events

The athletics field events consist of the jumping and throwing competitions. Most of these are organised into qualifying and final rounds, with only the final stages counting towards medal positions.

Decathlon

The decathlon events take place over two days. On day one, competitors take part in the 100 metres dash, long jump, shot put, high jump and 400 metres run. On day two, the athletes contest the 110 metre hurdles, discus, pole vault, javelin and 1,500 metres run. Points are awarded to athletes in each section of the competition. The medals are awarded to the athletes with the most points.

Heptathlon

The women's multi-event competition is the heptathlon and also takes place over two days. The 100 metre hurdles, shot put, high jump and 200 metres run are held on the first day with the long jump, javelin and 800 metres run on the second day. The scoring system is similar to that used in the decathlon.

High jump

High jumpers must take off from one foot as they attempt to jump over a thin bar balanced between two upright posts. Three successive failures result in a jumper being eliminated. The bar is raised until all the athletes have reached their limit. In the event of a tie, the winner is the competitor who has cleared the top height with the fewest failures at that height. If this does not separate the leading contestants, the one with the fewest failures at lower heights wins. If there is still a tie, a tie-break, or 'jump off', is held to decide the medal positions.

Pole vault

The men's pole vault competition is organised and decided in the same way as the high jump, except that competitors use a long pole to help them to clear much greater heights.

Maxim Tarassov (EUN), 1992 Olympic pole vault champion

Javier Sotomayor (Cuba), high jump gold medallist in Barcelona, 1992

Long jump

To make a valid jump, an athlete must not overstep the take-off board on the approach. A jump is measured from the board to the nearest impression in the sand made by the jumper. Each competitor has three jumps in the qualifying stage. Those who reach a certain standard proceed to the final stage. Only the jumps made in the final stage count towards medal placings, the winner being the competitor with the longest jump.

Triple jump

Also known as the 'hop, step and jump', the triple jump is similar to the long jump, except that the athlete jumps and lands on the same foot, then propels him/herself forward with that foot, landing on the other, and finally jumping, long jump-style, into a sand pit. Like the long jump, medal placings are awarded to the athletes with the longest jumps. There will be a women's triple jump competition for the first time at the Atlanta Olympics.

Men's field events		
Event	1992 winner and result	1996 winner and result
Decathlon	R. Zmelik (Czechoslovakia)	....
Winning score:	8611 points	....
Olympic record:	8847 points	New record? Yes / No
High jump	J. Sotomayor (Cuba)	....
Winning height:	2.34 metres	....
Olympic record:	2.38 metres	New record? Yes / No
Long jump	C. Lewis (United States)	....
Winning distance:	8.67 metres	....
Olympic record:	8.90 metres	New record? Yes / No
Triple jump	M. Conley (United States)	....
Winning distance:	18.17 metres	....
Olympic record:	18.17 metres	New record? Yes / No
Pole vault	M. Tarassov (EUN)	....
Winning height:	5.80 metres	....
Olympic record:	5.90 metres	New record? Yes / No
Discus	R. Ubartas (Lithuania)	....
Winning distance:	65.12 metres	....
Olympic record:	68.82 metres	New record? Yes / No
Javelin	J. Zelezny (Czechoslovakia)	....
Winning distance:	89.66 metres	....
Olympic record:	89.66 metres	New record? Yes / No
Shot put	M. Stulce (United States)	....
Winning distance:	21.70 metres	....
Olympic record:	22.47 metres	New record? Yes / No
Hammer	A. Abduvaliyev (EUN)	....
Winning distance:	82.54 metres	....
Olympic record:	84.80 metres	New record? Yes / No

Women's field events		
Event	1992 winner and result	1996 winner and result
Heptathlon	J. Joyner-Kersee (United States)	....
Winning score:	7044 points	....
Olympic record:	7291 points	New record? Yes / No
High jump	H. Henkel (Germany)	....
Winning height:	2.02 metres	....
Olympic record:	2.03 metres	New record? Yes / No
Long jump	H. Drechsler (Germany)	....
Winning distance:	7.14 metres	....
Olympic record:	7.40 metres	New record? Yes / No
Triple jump		
Winning distance:	New event for 1996	....
Discus	M. Marten (Cuba)	....
Winning distance:	70.06 metres	....
Olympic record:	70.30 metres	New record? Yes / No
Javelin	S. Renke (Germany)	....
Winning distance:	68.34 metres	....
Olympic record:	74.68 metres	New record? Yes / No
Shot put	S. Kriveleva (EUN)	....
Winning distance:	21.06 metres	....
Olympic record:	22.41 metres	New record? Yes / No

Throwing events consist of qualifying and final stages and contestants are given three attempts to qualify for the final. Throws aren't valid if the thrower steps out of the circle, or over the line for the javelin. Medals are awarded to athletes with the longest throws.

Javelin

When thrown, a javelin must land with its sharp end pointing downwards for a throw to count. Men's javelins weigh 800 grams, women's weigh 600 grams.

Hammer

The 'hammer' is a 7.26 kilogram metal ball attached to a grip by a spring steel wire not longer than 121.5 centimetres. It is possible for a hammer to be thrown over 80 metres. There is no women's hammer throwing competition.

Shot put

A 'shot' is a 7.26 kilogram metal ball, although women use a lighter 4 kilogram version. The shot must be 'put', that is, lifted from the contestant's shoulder, not thrown.

Discus

A discus weighs 2 kilograms (men's) or 1 kilogram (women's).

Silke Renke (Germany) winning gold at Barcelona 1992 in the javelin event

Badminton

Badminton was a new event at the Barcelona Olympics in 1992. This year's competition will consist of men's and women's singles and doubles matches with a mixed doubles competition added as a new event for 1996.

In the men's singles and both the men's and women's doubles events, each set is played over the best of three games up to 15 points. Women's singles is played up to 11 points. The competition is played on a knock-out basis until eight teams are left who go through to the quarter-finals. Semi-finals then the final follow, with both the losing semi-finalists receiving a bronze medal.

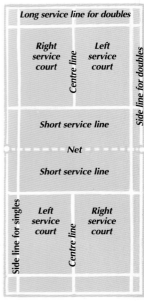

Back boundary line also long service line for singles

Long service line for doubles		
Right service court	Centre line	Left service court

Side line for doubles

Short service line

Net

Short service line

| Left service court | Centre line | Right service court |

Side line for singles

The singles court is not as wide as the doubles court, but in singles the service courts are longer than in doubles, as they stretch all the way back to the boundary line

Georgia State University – location for the badminton events at Atlanta 1996

Susi Susanti (Indonesia), 1992 Olympic gold medallist

Event	1992 winner	1996 winner
Women's		
Singles	S. Susanti (Indonesia)	....
Doubles	H-Y. Hwang and Y-S. Chung (S. Korea)	....
Men's		
Singles	A. B. Kusuma (Indonesia)	....
Doubles	M-S. Kim and J-B. Park (S. Korea)	....
Mixed		
Doubles	New event for 1996	....

DID YOU KNOW?

• Indonesia won its first ever Olympic gold medals during the badminton events in 1992.

• Zhao Jianhua (China) who finished fifth in the men's singles at Barcelona, was nicknamed Zhao 'Kapow' when he started playing badminton in 1985 because of his dynamic attacking style.

Baseball

Baseball was included as an 'exhibition sport' in the Olympics as early as 1912 but did not become a full Olympic event until the Barcelona Games in 1992.

Each player has three attempts to hit the ball thrown by the pitcher. The batter is out if he either fails to hit the ball after three strikes, hits the ball which is then caught by a fielder, is touched by the ball in the hand of a fielder while between bases, or if a fielder standing on a base catches the ball before the batter reaches the base. The batter scores a run by hitting the ball and trying to reach first, second and third base and then making it back to home base. If the batter achieves this in one move it is known as a 'home run'.

The competition will comprise preliminary rounds, semi-finals and a final. In the preliminary round, each team plays one match against all the other teams. The top four teams go through to cross-over semi-finals followed by a final. To decide the bronze medal position, a play-off between the losing semi-finalists is played.

Netherlands v Chinese Taipei – Barcelona, 1992

United States v Sweden – Stockholm, 1912

Event	1992 winner	1996 winner
Men's	Cuba	....

VENUE: ATLANTA-FULTON COUNTY STADIUM, OLYMPIC RING

Basketball

Since it was introduced to the modern Games in 1936, Olympic basketball has been dominated by the United States. In fact, it wasn't until the 1972 Games that the United States actually lost a game! On that occasion they were beaten 51-50 by the USSR.

The object of basketball is to pass and throw a ball through a circular hoop 3.05 metres above the ground. There is a hoop at each end of the court. The scoring is as follows: 2 points for a 'basket' from open play and 1 point for a basket from a free throw (penalty shot). Players are not allowed to carry the ball as they run but must bounce it along the ground as they move down the court.

The basketball competition is divided into preliminary rounds where the teams will be divided into two groups. Each team plays every other team in the group. In the men's competition the four teams from each group with the highest number of points go forward to the quarter-finals, while in the women's competition the top two teams from each group go on to the semi-finals.

A play-off is played to decide the bronze medal positions.

Michael Jordan (United States) passes his opponent from Spain with ease at the 1992 Olympics

DID YOU KNOW?
• The tallest medal winners in Olympic history are the basketball players Tommy Burleson (United States – silver medallist in 1972) and Arvidas Sabonis (USSR – gold medallist in 1988) who both measured 2.23 metres in height.

Event	1992 winner	1996 winner
Women's	EUN	....
Men's	United States	....

VENUE: GEORGIA DOME, OLYMPIC CENTER

Boxing

Boxing was included in the Ancient Olympics of 668BC, with the competitors wearing leather straps on their hands rather than boxing gloves. As the Games deteriorated in Roman times, metal studs were added. Later still, boxers wore metal 'knuckledusters'. The sport was introduced to the modern Games in 1904.

Olympic boxing contests involve twelve weight divisions organised on a knock-out basis right up to the final.

Each contest is boxed over three rounds of three minutes with a one minute break between rounds. Most of these bouts are decided on points, but it is possible for a boxer to win by a knockout or for the referee to stop a contest early for the safety of the loser.

Boxing is one of the few Olympic sports where the entrants aren't seeded. It is therefore possible for the two main favourites to meet in the first round.

The boxing arena at the Barcelona Olympics in 1992 hosted some exciting and challenging rounds

Michael Carruth (Ireland), gold medallist in the welterweight event at the Olympic Games, 1992

DID YOU KNOW?

• More than twenty World Professional Boxing Champions previously won Olympic gold medals as amateurs. Some of the most famous of these are Muhammad Ali (formerly Cassius Clay), Joe Frazier, Leon Spinks and Lennox Lewis.

Weight division	1992 winner	1996 winner
Under 48 kilograms **Light flyweight**	R. Marcelo (Cuba)	....
Under 51 kilograms **Flyweight**	C. Choi (N. Korea)	....
Under 54 kilograms **Bantamweight**	J. Casamayor (Cuba)	....
Under 57 kilograms **Featherweight**	A. Tews (Germany)	....
Under 60 kilograms **Lightweight**	O. De La Boya (United States)	....
Under 63.5 kilograms **Light welterweight**	H. Vinent (Cuba)	....
Under 67 kilograms **Welterweight**	M. Carruth (Ireland)	....
Under 71 kilograms **Light middleweight**	J. Lemus (Cuba)	....
Under 75 kilograms **Middleweight**	A. Hernandez (Cuba)	....
Under 81 kilograms **Light heavyweight**	T. May (Germany)	....
Under 91 kilograms **Heavyweight**	F. Savon (Cuba)	....
Over 91 kilograms **Super heavyweight**	R. Balado (Cuba)	....

Oscar De La Boya (United States) on his way to winning gold in the Olympic lightweight event, 1992

Rogelio Marcelo (Cuba), gold medallist in the light flyweight event at Barcelona, 1992

Canoeing

Canoeing was first introduced to the modern Games at the 1936 Olympics in Berlin. There are two types of canoeing in the Games – kayak and Canadian.

Kayak

Both men and women compete in the kayak singles, doubles and fours events using a paddle with a blade at each end. The canoeist must use the left-hand blade on the left side and the right-hand blade on the right side of the kayak alternately.

The kayak paddler sits inside the kayak, with legs outstretched under the deck

Canadian

In these events, the canoeist has a paddle with one blade which he uses alternately on either side of his canoe. There are no women's events in Canadian canoeing.

The Canadian canoe is usually open, although a spraydeck may be fitted. This type of canoe is used in the Canadian slalom

In the slalom races, in both the kayak and Canadian events, the canoeists have to negotiate a series of gates defined by poles hanging over the course in two timed runs. Time penalties are added for any missed gates where a competitor doesn't succeed in getting at least their head and shoulders between the poles without touching them. The better of the two runs counts, with the top three competitors in each event winning the medals.

In the sprint races, the competitors must canoe down a set course in the fastest time possible, with the medals awarded for the quickest times.

This year's slalom course should prove as challenging as in 1992

DID YOU KNOW?

• The closest race in Olympic canoeing history was between Finland and Sweden in the 1,000 metres kayak pairs at Helsinki in 1952. The judges awarded the race to Finland after studying a photograph of the finish, but they could not separate the teams' times of 3 minutes 51.1 seconds.

Event	1992 winner	1996 winner
Women's kayak		
Slalom (singles)	E. Micheler (Germany)	....
500 metres (singles)	B. Schmidt (Germany)	....
500 metres (pairs)	Germany	....
500 metres (fours)	Hungary	....
Men's kayak		
Slalom (singles)	P. Ferrazzi (Italy)	....
500 metres (singles)	M. Kolehmainen (Finland)	....
1,000 metres (singles)	C. Robinson (Australia)	....
500 metres (pairs)	Germany	....
1,000 metres (pairs)	Germany	....
1,000 metres (fours)	Germany	....
Men's Canadian		
Slalom (singles)	L. Pollert (Czechoslovakia)	....
500 metres (singles)	N. Boukhalov (Bulgaria)	....
1,000 metres (singles)	N. Boukhalov (Bulgaria)	....
Slalom (pairs)	United States	....
500 metres (pairs)	EUN	....
1,000 metres (pairs)	Germany	....

Canoeists test their strength and ability at the 1992 Olympic Games

Joaquin Garcia (Costa Rica) battles against the elements in the slalom kayak finals at Barcelona, 1992

Cycling

Although cycling was a part of the first modern Olympic Games in 1896, women's events in the sport did not begin until 1984.

There are six different types of cycling events:

Pursuit

Both individual and team pursuit races are held over 4,000 metres. The competing cyclists start at opposite sides of the track and the aim is to catch up with your opponent or the opposing team of four. If this is not achieved, the fastest times decide the winner or winners as with the road races and the sprints.

Road race

Held on the road over about 195 kilometres (men) and 81 kilometres (women), these races are for individual competitors.

Sprint

This individual race is held over four laps of the track and is usually contested by two or three cyclists, but only the time for the last 200 metres counts – the earlier parts of the race are used to gain a favourable position.

Time trial

The time trial events involve cyclists setting off at intervals and racing against the clock. The fastest time over the various courses wins the race.

Points race

These races are held over 200 laps of the track – 50 kilometres. Every eighth lap the first cyclist to cross the line scores five points, the second scores three, the third scores two and the fourth scores one. Double points are scored on both the 100th and the final lap. The competitor with the most points at the end of the race is the winner.

Mountain bike

New for Atlanta 1996, competitors will use mountain bikes to ride over rough terrain instead of regular racing bicycles in this men-only event. Again, the fastest time decides the medal placings.

DID YOU KNOW?
• In 1992 Chris Boardman's bike was a revolutionary prototype. This winning bike had just one bar and no triangle and it was built from special carbon fibre to make it lighter.

Chris Boardman (Great Britain) smashes the 4,000 metres pursuit record at the 1992 Olympic final

VENUE: STONE MOUNTAIN VELODROME, OLYMPIC PARK AT STONE MOUNTAIN

Event	1992 winner	1996 winner
Women's		
Individual pursuit	P. Rossner (Germany)	....
Road race	K. Watt (Australia)	....
Sprint	E. Salumae (Estonia)	....
Road time trial	New event for 1996	....
Track event	New event for 1996	....
Men's		
Individual pursuit	C. Boardman (Great Britain)	....
Team pursuit	Germany	....
Road race	F. Casartelli (Italy)	....
Sprint	J. Fiedler (Germany)	....
1,000 metre time trial	J. Moreno (Spain)	....
Road time trial	G. Lombardi (Italy)	....
Mountain bike	New event for 1996	....

Equestrian

The first equestrian event in the modern Olympics was the show jumping competition in 1900. Nowadays three equestrian events are held at each Games and are unusual in that men and women compete against one another on an equal basis.

Show jumping

Competitors have to jump a course of between ten and twelve obstacles in two qualifying rounds. The highest obstacle is 1.6 metres, the widest is 2.2 metres. Faults count against the competitors if they knock any of the obstacles down.

In the team event, four riders jump a similar qualifying course. The twelve best teams jump against the clock over a shorter course. The three best scores of the four riders count. Medal positions are awarded to the team/individual with the least number of faults.

DID YOU KNOW?

• Reiner Klimke (Germany) won five gold medals in five separate Olympic Games over a 24 year period between 1964 and 1988 in the dressage competition.
• Over the years Germany has proved itself highly successful in the field of dressage.

Event	1992 winner	1996 winner
Show jumping		
Individual	L. Beerbaum & Classic Touch (Germany)	....
Team	Netherlands	....
Dressage		
Individual	N. Uphoff & Rembrandt (Germany)	....
Team	Germany	....
Three-day event		
Individual	M. Ryan & Kibah Tic Toc (Australia)	....
Team	Australia	....

VENUE: GEORGIA INTERNATIONAL HORSE PARK, CONYERS-ROCKDALE COUNTY

Fencing

Fencing has been included in the modern Games since they began in 1896. Women have been competing since 1924. Great Britain won its last gold medal in the fencing events back in 1964 when Bill Hoskyns took a silver in Tokyo.

There are three swords used in Olympic fencing: the foil, the epee and the sabre. Men and women compete in both team and individual fencing events, but there is no women's sabre competition.

To score, the fencer must hit certain target areas on the opponent's body. The competition is based on a knockout basis. In the qualifying rounds a fencer must score five hits to win. In later rounds, a fencer must win two out of three fights against the same opponent in order to progress through the competition to the semi-finals and the final.

Foil
This sword has a flexible rectangular blade and a blunt point. Scoring is achieved by touching the opponent's body between the collar and hipbones with the point of the blade.

Epee
An epee sword has a rigid triangular blade with a point covered by a cone. Scoring is achieved when only the tip of the sword touches any part of the body including the face.

Sabre
This sword has a flexible triangular blade with a blunt point. Scoring is achieved when the point or the blade touches a part of the body above the waist including the face.

Giovanna Trillini (Italy) encounters Huifeng Wang (China) in the individual foil competition – Barcelona, 1992

DID YOU KNOW?
• Woman fencer Kerstin Palm (Sweden) competed in seven Olympic Games from 1964 to 1988. This is a record attendance for any female at the Games in any sport.

Event	1992 winner	1996 winner
Women's		
Foil – individual	G. Trillini (Italy)	....
Foil – team	Italy	....
Epee – individual	New event for 1996	....
Epee – team	New event for 1996	....
Men's		
Foil – individual	P. Omnes (France)	....
Foil – team	Germany	....
Epee – individual	E. Srecki (France)	....
Epee – team	Germany	....
Sabre – individual	B. Szabo (Hungary)	....
Sabre – team	EUN	....

VENUE: GEORGIA WORLD CONGRESS CENTER, OLYMPIC CENTER

Football

Football has been part of the Olympics throughout the history of the modern Games with the first official tournament held at the 1900 Games in France. Great Britain, represented by Upton Park FC, won the gold medal on that occasion.

In football, teams are divided into groups of four with each team playing a match against each of the others. The teams are awarded 2 points for a win, 1 point for a draw and 0 points if they lose.

The top two teams in each group then go forward to a knockout stage comprising quarter-finals, semi-finals and a final.

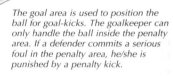

Kwame Ayen (Ghana) helping his team to secure the bronze medal in the 1992 Olympics

The goal area is used to position the ball for goal-kicks. The goalkeeper can only handle the ball inside the penalty area. If a defender commits a serious foul in the penalty area, he/she is punished by a penalty kick.

Spain v Ghana – Olympic Games, 1992

DID YOU KNOW?
• There is no British football team in the Olympic Games because the Football Associations of England, Scotland, Wales, the Republic of Ireland and Northern Ireland believe a British team might endanger the separate existence of English, Scottish, Welsh and Irish teams in future World Cups.

Event	1992 winner	1996 winner
Men's	Spain	....
Women's	New event for 1996	....

VENUE: OLYMPIC STADIUM, OLYMPIC RING

Gymnastics

Gymnastics have been part of the modern Games since they began in 1896. Gymnasts are among the competitors who hold the greatest number of medals. This is a result of the high number of events.

The gymnastics competition is held over three days. On the first two days all gymnasts perform one compulsory and one optional exercise in each event. The men's events are the floor exercises, pommel horse, rings, horse vault, parallel bars and horizontal bar. The women's events are the floor exercises, asymmetric bars, horse vault and balance beam. All competitors receive marks out of 10 from a panel of judges for each exercise at each event. The highest scores of the top five gymnasts from each country decide the team medal positions.

The best 36 gymnasts then go forward to the individual all-round competition. Here, they perform a further optional exercise at each event and this score is added to their previous average to determine the all-round champion.

Finally, the eight gymnasts with the best scores in each event perform one last exercise in the individual final for that event. These new scores are added to each competitor's previous average mark to decide the individual event medal placings.

Vitali Chtcherbo (EUN) swept the board with five gold medals in Barcelona, 1992

Women's exercises		
Event	1992 winner	1996 winner
Asymmetric bars	L. Lu (China)	....
Beam	T. Lyssenko (EUN)	....
Floor	L. Milosovici (Romania)	....
Horse vault	H. Onodi (Hungary)	....
All-round	T. Goutsou (EUN)	....
Team	EUN	....
Rhythmic all-round Individual	A. Timoshenko (EUN)	....
Team	New event for 1996	....

Men's exercises

Event	1992 winner	1996 winner
Floor	X. Li (China)	....
Horizontal bar	T. Dimas (United States)	....
Parallel bars	V. Chtcherbo (EUN)	....
Pommel horse	V. Chtcherbo (EUN)	....
Rings	V. Chtcherbo (EUN)	....
Horse vault	V. Chtcherbo (EUN)	....
All-round	V. Chtcherbo (EUN)	....
Team	EUN	....

Since 1984 there has also been a rhythmic gymnastics competition. This is a separate competition from the more traditional gymnastic events and involves the use of the following props: ribbon, hoop, ball and clubs. Rhythmic gymnasts face a preliminary competition using each piece of equipment. Only the top twelve go through to the final where the medals are awarded to the highest scorers.

DID YOU KNOW?

• One of the most remarkable performances in Olympic gymnastics history was by the American George Eyser at the 1904 Olympic Games. He won six medals, including three gold, despite having a wooden leg!

Li Lu (China) giving a gold medal performance on the asymmetric bars – Barcelona 1992

Alexandra Timoshenko (EUN) puts in a winning performance in the rhythmic gymnastics at the Olympics, 1992

Handball

The current game of indoor seven-a-side handball was first played at the modern Games in 1972, with the women's events starting in 1976. It was, however, first introduced to the modern Games in 1936 when it was played as an outdoor, eleven-a-side game.

The aim of handball is to throw a ball into a goal to score. However, a player is only allowed to hold the ball, if caught two-handed, for a maximum of three seconds before he or she must shoot or pass. Similarly a player may only take a maximum of three steps while holding the ball. Only shots made outside the goal area and which pass the keeper into the goal count.

Twelve men's teams compete in two groups of six in the men's events, and eight women's teams compete in two groups of four in the women's events. Two points are awarded for a win, 1 for a draw and 0 for a loss. The top two teams from each group go to cross-over semi-finals, the winners go forward to the final. A play-off is played for the bronze medal.

Event	1992 winner	1996 winner
Women's	S. Korea	....
Men's	EUN	....

DID YOU KNOW?
• The highest handball win in Olympic history was Yugoslavia's 44-10 defeat of Kuwait in 1980.

VENUE: GEORGIA WORLD CONGRESS CENTER, OLYMPIC CENTER

Hockey

Hockey first featured in the modern Games in 1908 and has been part of the Games on all but two occasions (1912 and 1924) since.

Hockey is played between two teams of eleven players over two halves, each of which lasts 35 minutes, and is similar to the rules of football. The teams are divided into two groups and the top two teams from each group go forward to the semi-finals. The competition then enters a knockout phase to decide the medal positions.

Germany v Great Britain – Barcelona 1992

DID YOU KNOW?
• The first Olympic hockey champions were England in 1908 when they beat Ireland 8-1.

Event	1992 winner	1996 winner
Women's	Spain	....
Men's	Germany	....

VENUE: HERNDON STADIUM/MORRIS BROWN COLLEGE, OLYMPIC CENTER

Judo

Judo was first introduced to the modern Games in 1964. It is an unarmed combat sport based on the principles of self-defence. Women's judo was first introduced to the Olympics in 1992 when Great Britain won a total of three medals across seven events.

Nikki Fairbrother (Great Britain) shows skill and strength at Barcelona, 1992. She went on to take the silver medal in the lightweight event

Judo matches last a maximum of five minutes but can be ended by the score of an 'ippon' by one of the combatants. An ippon is scored by either a clean, forceful throw or by a hold, keeping your opponent under your control for 30 seconds. An ippon can also be scored by a submission to a strangle or a lock applied against the elbow. If no ippon is scored, then lesser scores decide the winner. In the event of a tie, the referee and two judges determine which competitor has displayed superiority.

The actual competition is based on knock-out draws with competitors being eliminated until the gold, silver and bronze medals have been awarded.

Women's events		
Event	1992 winner	1996 winner
Under 48 kilograms **Extra-lightweight**	C. Nowak (France)	....
Under 52 kilograms **Half-lightweight**	A. Muñoz Martinez (Spain)	....
Under 56 kilograms **Lightweight**	M. Blasco Soto (Spain)	....
Under 61 kilograms **Half-middleweight**	C. Fleury (France)	....
Under 66 kilograms **Middleweight**	O. Reve Jimenez (Cuba)	....
Under 72 kilograms **Half-heavyweight**	M-J. Kim (S. Korea)	....
Over 72 kilograms **Heavyweight**	X. Zhuang (China)	....

VENUE: GEORGIA WORLD CONGRESS CENTER, OLYMPIC CENTER

Men's events

Event	1992 winner	1996 winner
Under 60 kilograms **Extra-lightweight**	N. Gousseinov (EUN)	....
Under 65 kilograms **Half-lightweight**	R. Sampaio Cardoso (Brazil)	....
Under 71 kilograms **Lightweight**	T. Koga (Japan)	....
Under 78 kilograms **Half-middleweight**	H. Yoshida (Japan)	....
Under 86 kilograms **Middleweight**	W. Legien (Poland)	....
Under 95 kilograms **Half-heavyweight**	A. Kovacs (Hungary)	....
Over 95 kilograms **Heavyweight**	D. Khakhaleichvili (EUN)	....

Hidehiko Yoshida (Japan) throws Jason Morris (United States) to win gold in the half-middleweight event – Barcelona, 1992

DID YOU KNOW?

• Angelo Parisi won Olympic judo medals for two different countries – a bronze in 1972 for Great Britain and a gold and a silver for France in 1980.

Modern Pentathlon

The modern pentathlon was introduced to the modern Olympics in 1912 and is so called because there was a pentathlon competition in the Ancient Olympics. It was introduced at the insistence of Spartan warriors who thought that there should be a test to discover the 'supreme athlete'.

The modern pentathlon comprises show jumping (over 15 obstacles), fencing (epee), shooting (pistol or revolver at 25 metres), swimming (300 metres freestyle) and cross-country running (4,000 metres).

Points are awarded for each section of the competition and the winner is the athlete or the team with the most points. Each team is made up of four men, although only three competitors will line up at the start.

Event	1992 winner	1996 winner
Individual	A. Skrzypaszek (Poland)	....
Team	Poland	....

DID YOU KNOW?
• The pentathlon of the Ancient Olympics included javelin, discus, jumping, running and wrestling.

VENUE: VARIOUS SITES, OLYMPIC PARK AT STONE MOUNTAIN

Rowing

The first rowing event in the modern Olympics was held at the 1900 Games. Women's rowing events were introduced in 1976. Olympic rowing was standardised in 1988 and all events, both men's and women's, are now held over 2,000 metres.

DID YOU KNOW?
• The youngest gold medallist in Olympic history was almost certainly the French boy who coxed the winning Dutch pair in 1900. Sadly, the boy's identity is unknown but he is believed to have been between seven and ten years old.

Gold medallists Greg and John Searle with their cox Garry Herbert (Great Britain) – Olympics, 1992

Rowing has probably made more progress in equipment than any other sport and it is extremely difficult to keep the competition athletic rather than technological. There are six events for the men and five events for the women with two categories – sweep rowing (coxless pairs, fours and eights) and sculling, the fastest individual/teams in each event winning the medals.

VENUE: STONE MOUNTAIN LAKE, OLYMPIC PARK AT STONE MOUNTAIN

Women's events

Event	1992 winner	1996 winner
Coxless fours	Canada	....
Single sculls	Romania	....
Double sculls	Germany	....
Eights	Canada	....
Quadruple sculls	Germany	....

Men's events

Event	1992 winner	1996 winner
Coxless pairs	Great Britain	....
Coxless fours	Australia	....
Single sculls	Germany	....
Double sculls	Australia	....
Eights	Canada	....
Quadruple sculls	Germany	....

Shooting

The founder of the modern Olympic Games – Baron Pierre de Coubertin – was an enthusiastic pistol shot and so, not surprisingly, shooting has been included in the modern Olympics since 1896. There has been a wide variety of shooting over the years which has featured in all except the 1904 and 1928 Games.

Kab-Soon Yeo (South Korea) aims for gold at the Olympic Games, 1992

DID YOU KNOW?

• The record number of shooting medals won by a single competitor is 11. Carl Osburn (United States) won five gold, four silver and two bronze medals between the years 1912 and 1924.

Women's events

Event	1992 winner	1996 winner
Air pistol	M. Logvinenko (EUN)	....
Sport pistol	M. Logvinenko (EUN)	....
Air rifle	K-S. Yeo (S. Korea)	....
Rifle three positions	L. Meili (United States)	....
Double trap	New event for 1996	....

Of the 15 shooting events, six are shot using rifles, five using pistols and four with shotguns.

Each event has a qualifying stage of between 40 and 150 shots. The leading four, six or eight shooters fire again in a shorter final, and have 10 shots in rifle and pistol, but more in shotgun.

In air rifle and air pistol, men have 105 minutes to fire 60 shots and women have 75 minutes to fire 40 shots at a target 10 metres away. The bulls-eye on the air rifle target is only half a millimetre wide, smaller then a pinhead.

Rapid fire pistol competitors fire at five targets 25 metres away, and have

Competitors showing great concentration in the rifle shooting event, Barcelona, 1992

eight, six or four seconds, one at each target, depending on the stage of the competition.

The shotgun events involve shooting at saucer-shaped clay discs as they fly through the air.

Men's events

Event	1992 winner	1996 winner
Air pistol	Y. Wang (China)	....
Air rifle	I. Fedkine (EUN)	....
Free pistol	K. Lukaichik (EUN)	....
Rapid fire pistol	R. Schumann (Germany)	....
Rifle three positions	G. Petikiane (EUN)	....
Rifle prone	E-C. Lee (South Korea)	....
Running target	M. Jakosits (Germany)	....
Skeet	New event for 1996	....
Trap	New event for 1996	....
Double trap	New event for 1996	....

Softball

Softball was devised about 1887, but its first official appearance at the Olympics will be at Atlanta 1996. There are several forms of softball, but 'Women's Fastpitch' will be featured at Atlanta. There is no men's event at the Olympics.

DID YOU KNOW?
- A softball thrown underhand by a top woman pitcher travels just as fast as a baseball thrown by a Major League pitcher.

Softball is a form of baseball played with similar equipment and rules but with a larger ball. The other main differences are that a softball field is smaller (by about a third) and the pitcher (bowler) throws the ball underhand.

Eight teams will play a round-robin tournament at the Games. The top four teams will then advance to the semi-finals and finals. The losing semi-finalists will have a play-off for the bronze medal.

Event	1992 winner	1996 winner
Women's	New event for 1996	....

VENUE: GOLDEN PARK, COLUMBUS, GEORGIA

Swimming and Diving

Swimming has been a part of the modern Olympics since 1896. Women's events began in 1912. In the early modern Games, swimming took place in natural surroundings, for example in the sea or in lakes. The 50 metre pool was first used in 1924.

Men and women compete separately in a variety of events over varying distances using four different strokes – freestyle (usually called the crawl), breaststroke, backstroke and butterfly. The medley events combine all four strokes swum over four equal distances.

Depending on the number of entrants in each event, anywhere between five and ten heats are held. The winner of each heat progresses through to the final from which the medals are decided.

Alexandre Popov (EUN) powers through the water to take the 50 metres and 100 metres freestyle gold medals – Barcelona, 1992

VENUE: GEORGIA TECH NATATORIUM, OLYMPIC RING

Event	1992 winner and time	1996 winner and time
Women's freestyle **50 metres**	W. Yang (China)	....
Winning time:	0:24:79	....
Olympic record:	0:24:79	New record? Yes / No
100 metres	Y. Zhuang (China)	....
Winning time:	0:54:64	....
Olympic record:	0:54:64	New record? Yes / No
200 metres	N. Haislett (United States)	....
Winning time:	1:57:90	....
Olympic record:	1:57:65	New record? Yes / No
400 metres	D. Hase (Germany)	....
Winning time:	4:07:18	....
Olympic record:	4:03:85	New record? Yes / No
800 metres	J. Evans (United States)	....
Winning time:	8:25:52	....
Olympic record:	8:20:20	New record? Yes / No
4 x 100 metres	United States	....
Winning time:	3:39:46	....
Olympic record:	3:39:46	New record? Yes / No
4 x 200 metres	New event for 1996	....
Winning time:		....
Women's breaststroke **100 metres**	E. Roudkovskaia (EUN)	....
Winning time:	1:08:00	....
Olympic record:	1:07:95	New record? Yes / No
200 metres	K. Iwasaki (Japan)	....
Winning time:	2:26:65	....
Olympic record:	2:26:65	New record? Yes / No
Women's butterfly **100 metres**	H. Qian (China)	....
Winning time:	0:58:62	....
Olympic record:	0:58:62	New record? Yes / No
200 metres	S. Sanders (United States)	....
Winning time:	2:08:67	....
Olympic record:	2:06:90	New record? Yes / No
Women's backstroke **100 metres**	K. Egerszegi (Hungary)	....
Winning time:	1:00:68	....
Olympic record:	1:00:68	New record? Yes / No
200 metres	K. Egerszegi (Hungary)	....
Winning time:	2:07:06	....
Olympic record:	2:07:06	New record? Yes / No

Event	1992 winner and time	1996 winner and time
Men's freestyle		
50 metres	A. Popov (EUN)	....
Winning time:	0:21:91	....
Olympic record:	0:21:91	New record? Yes / No
100 metres	A. Popov (EUN)	....
Winning time:	0:49:02	....
Olympic record	0:48:63	New record? Yes / No
200 metres	E. Sadovyi (EUN)	....
Winning time:	1:46:70	....
Olympic record:	1:46:70	New record? Yes / No
400 metres	E. Sadovyi (EUN)	....
Winning time:	3:45:00	....
Olympic record:	3:45:00	New record? Yes / No
1,500 metres	K. Perkins (Australia)	....
Winning time:	14:43:48	....
Olympic record:	14:43:48	New record? Yes / No
4 x 100 metres	United States	....
Winning time:	3:16:74	....
Olympic record:	3:16:53	New record? Yes / No
4 x 200 metres	EUN	....
Winning time:	7:11:95	....
Olympic record:	7:11:95	New record? Yes / No
Men's breaststroke		
100 metres	N. W. Diebel (United States)	....
Winning time:	1:01:50	....
Olympic record:	1:01:50	New record? Yes / No
200 metres	M. Barrowman (United States)	....
Winning time:	2:10:16	....
Olympic record:	2:10:16	New record? Yes / No
Men's butterfly		
100 metres	P. Morales (United States)	....
Winning time:	0:53:32	....
Olympic record:	0:53:00	New record? Yes / No
200 metres	M. Stewart (United States)	....
Winning time:	1:56:26	....
Olympic record:	1:56:26	New record? Yes / No
Men's backstroke		
100 metres	M. Tewksbury (Canada)	....
Winning time:	0:53:98	....
Olympic record:	0:53:98	New record? Yes / No
200 metres	M. Lopez-Zubero (Spain)	....
Winning time:	1:58:47	....
Olympic record:	1:58:47	New record? Yes / No

Event	1992 winner and time	1996 winner and time
Women's medley		
200 metres	L. Lin (China)	....
Winning time:	2:11:65	....
Olympic record:	2:11:65	New record? Yes / No
400 metres	E. Egerszegi (Hungary)	....
Winning time:	4:36:54	....
Olympic record:	4:36:29	New record? Yes / No
4 x 100 metres	United States	....
Winning time:	4:02:54	....
Olympic record:	4:02:54	New record? Yes / No
Men's medley		
200 metres	T. Darnyi (Hungary)	....
Winning time:	2:00:76	....
Olympic record:	2:00:17	New record? Yes / No
400 metres	T. Darnyi (Hungary)	....
Winning time:	4:14:23	....
Olympic record:	4:14:23	New record? Yes / No
4 x 100 metres	United States	....
Winning time:	3:36:93	....
Olympic record:	3:36:93	New record? Yes / No

Kerry Shacklock and Laila Vakil (Great Britain) performing with grace and style – Olympic Games, 1992

DID YOU KNOW?
• The United States dominates the Olympic swimming and diving events. In swimming they have won more than a third of all the medals, and in diving they have won more medals than all the other countries put together.

Synchronised swimming

This sport was first introduced to the Olympics at the Los Angeles Games in 1984. Competitors must perform four compulsory movements of varying degrees of difficulty and a free routine set to music which lasts for four minutes.

There have previously been solo and duet events but in Atlanta 1996 there will only be a team event. Like diving, synchronised swimming is marked by judges out of a maximum of ten points, the medals being awarded to the highest scorers.

Event	1992 winner	1996 winner
Synchronised swimming Women's team	New for 1996	....

Diving

Springboard and platform (highboard) events for men and women make up the Olympic diving competition. The number of dives which each competitor performs is 11 for men's springboard, 11 for men's platform, 8 for women's platform and 10 for women's springboard. Each one is marked out of ten by a panel of judges. The highest and lowest marked dives are then discounted and the remaining scores are added together and then multiplied by a tariff value which takes into account the technical difficulty of the dives. These final figures provide the medal placings. There are over 80 recognised competition dives and each one carries a different degree of difficulty grading.

Shuwei Sun (China) will be hoping to repeat his 1992 Olympic gold medal performance in Atlanta this year

Nicole Haislett (United States) gets a good start in the 200 metres freestyle event, Olympic Games, 1992. She went on to take the gold medal

Mark Lenzi (United States) dives to win his gold medal, Olympic Games, 1992, in the men's springboard final

Event	1992 winner	1996 winner
Diving		
Women's platform	M. Fu (China)	....
Women's springboard	M. Gao (China)	....
Men's platform	S. Sun (China)	....
Men's springboard	M. Lenzi (United States)	....

Table Tennis

Table tennis was first introduced as an official Olympic event at the 1988 Games in Seoul with men's and women's singles and doubles games. Table tennis bats have undergone many changes over the years, helping the sport to be fast, dynamic and exciting with a mixture of styles and tactics.

A qualifying group stage is played first, with the best-placed competitors going forward to the knockout stage with quarter-finals, semi-finals and a final. Bronze medals are awarded to both losing semi-finalists.

Group matches are the best of three games and the later knockout matches are the best of five games. Games are played up to 21 points or beyond if a 2 point lead has not been achieved.

Jan Waldner (Sweden) on his way to winning the gold medal in the men's singles event – Barcelona 1992

Table tennis is an exciting sport to watch because of the speed and energy shown by the competitors

The elements that have changed the game of table tennis over the years have been the different materials attached to the surface of the bat. The blade may be of any weight, size or shape but must be made of wood of even thickness, flat, rigid and unperforated.

The table tennis table is 0.76 metres off the ground, 1.52 metres wide and 2.74 metres long with a net only 0.16 metres high.

Event		1992 winner	1996 winner
Women's	Singles	Y. Deng (China)	....
	Doubles	China	....
Men's	Singles	J. Waldner (Sweden)	....
	Doubles	China	....

DID YOU KNOW?

• China has dominated the medal tables in the past two Olympic Games, winning five out of a possible eight gold medals.

VENUE: GEORGIA WORLD CONGRESS CENTER, OLYMPIC CENTER

Tennis

Although tennis was one of the sports included in the very first modern Olympic Games in 1896, there were no Olympic tennis events between 1924 and 1988.

As in tennis Grand Slam tournaments, male competitors play five set matches whereas for women the matches are the best of three sets. Tie-breaks come into play in every set except the final set. To win the final set, a player must pull two games clear of his or her opponent. There are no mixed doubles in the Olympic Games.

The competition consists of qualifying rounds, quarter-finals, semi-finals and a final played on clay courts.

Jennifer Capriati (United States) showing true champion spirit as she takes the gold in the women's singles event – Olympic Games, 1992

Steffi Graf (Germany) showing athletic form at the Olympics, Barcelona, 1992

Michael Stich and Boris Becker (Germany) proudly presenting their Olympic gold medals after winning the men's doubles event – Barcelona, 1992

Event		1992 winner	1996 winner
Women's	**Singles**	J. Capriati (United States)	....
	Doubles	United States	....
Men's	**Singles**	M. Rosset (Switzerland)	....
	Doubles	Germany	....

DID YOU KNOW?

• The first tennis gold medallist was Irish-born John Pius Boland from Great Britain in 1896. He happened to be in Athens at the time of the Games and only entered the competition at the last minute.

VENUE: STONE MOUNTAIN TENNIS CENTER, OLYMPIC PARK AT STONE MOUNTAIN

Volleyball

Volleyball is played indoors and was first played at the modern Olympics in 1964. At Atlanta '96, outdoor beach volleyball will be introduced for the first time.

Brazil v Japan – Olympic Games, 1992

Teams have six members and points are scored when one side fails to return the ball successfully over the net and into the court after a maximum of three touches. Teams only score points on their serves and the winning target is 15 with a 2 point lead. Each match is the best of five sets.

The competition consists of qualifying rounds, quarter-finals, semi-finals and a final to decide the medal positions.

Event	1992 winner	1996 winner
Women's		
Indoor	Cuba	....
Beach	New event for 1996	....
Men's		
Indoor	Brazil	....
Beach	New event for 1996	....

DID YOU KNOW?

• Between 1964 and 1980 the men's team from the former Soviet Union lost only four of their 39 matches.

VENUE: OMNI, OLYMPIC CENTER

Water Polo

Water polo has been part of the modern Games since 1900 when the event was won by Great Britain.

Water polo is a demanding team game played by two teams of seven players, one of whom is the goalkeeper. The competition takes place in a pool measuring 33.3 metres by 25 metres and at least 1.80 metres deep – the players are not allowed to touch the bottom during play.

Italy v Spain in the final – Barcelona, 1992

DID YOU KNOW?

• The 1936 water polo match between Hungary and the former Soviet Union, had to be abandoned when the referee decided it was becoming 'a boxing match underwater'.

VENUE: ATLANTA UNIVERSITY COMPLEX, OLYMPIC CENTER

The game itself is divided into four periods of five minutes. The object of the game is to pass the ball and throw it into the goal of the opposition. The teams taking part in the competition are divided into two groups. Each team plays every other team in their group and the top two from each group then play in a knock-out competition to decide the medal positions.

Event	1992 winner	1996 winner
Men's	Italy	....

Weightlifting

Weightlifting was part of the first modern Games in 1896. International competitions exist for female weightlifters, but women do not take part at the Games.

There are ten different weight classes. Competitors have to lift as heavy a weight as possible using two distinct techniques – the 'snatch' and the 'jerk'. The snatch is performed by lifting a weight directly above the competitor's head in one movement. The jerk is a two-stage lift, requiring the competitor to bring the weight up to his shoulders and then lift it over his head.

Weightlifters are allowed three snatch attempts and three jerk attempts at each weight. The winner is the competitor who lifts the greatest total of weight using both techniques. If there is a tie, the lightest weightlifter is judged to have made the greater effort and is declared the winner.

The strength and determination of Israel Militossian (EUN) assured him the gold medal in the lightweight event – Olympic Games, 1992

Weight division	1992 winner	1996 winner
Under 52 kilograms **Flyweight**	I. Ivanov (Bulgaria)	....
Under 56 kilograms **Bantamweight**	B-K. Chun (S. Korea)	....
Under 60 kilograms **Featherweight**	N. Suleymanoglu (Turkey)	....
Under 67.5 kilograms **Lightweight**	I. Militossian (EUN)	....
Under 75 kilograms **Middleweight**	F. Kassapu (EUN)	....
Under 82.5 kilograms **Light heavyweight**	P. Dimas (Greece)	....
Under 90 kilograms **Middle heavyweight**	K. Kakhiachvili (EUN)	....
Under 100 kilograms **100 kilogram**	V. Tregoubov (EUN)	....
Under 110 kilograms **Heavyweight**	R. Weller (Germany)	....
Over 110 kilograms **Super heavyweight**	A. Kourlovitch (EUN)	....

Pyrrus Dimas (Greece) lifts for victory and gets the gold medal in the light heavyweight event – Barcelona 1992

DID YOU KNOW?

• The weightlifting silver medallist in the light heavyweight division at the 1948 Olympics was Harold Sakata. He later became famous by playing the role of the villainous Oddjob in the James Bond film 'Goldfinger'.

The weight proved too much for Cedric Plancon (France) who despite great effort finished ninth in the middle heavyweight event – Olympic Games, 1992

Wrestling

Wrestling was the most popular sport in the Ancient Olympics and has featured in all but one (1990) of the modern Games. There are two types of Olympic wrestling—Freestyle and Greco-Roman. The use of feet and the holding of your opponent below the hips are banned in Greco-Roman. In 1900, wrestling at the Games was of the Freestyle variety only. Both types of wrestling have been on the programme since 1908.

All wrestling bouts last five minutes and are fought out on a 12 metre square mat. Points are scored as a result of 'holds', 'positions of advantage' and 'near-throws'. A successful 'fall' ends the bout, as does a 12 point lead at any time during the bout. Otherwise, the leader on points at the end of five minutes is the winner. In the event of a draw, the referee extends the bout until another point is scored. When there are only three wrestlers remaining in the competition, the medals are awarded, taking into account each wrestler's penalty points collected throughout the competition.

Freestyle		
Division	1992 winner	1996 winner
Under 48 kilograms **Light flyweight**	I. Kim (N. Korea)	....
Under 52 kilograms **Flyweight**	H. Li (N. Korea)	....
Under 57 kilograms **Bantamweight**	A. Puerto (Cuba)	....
Under 62 kilograms **Featherweight**	J. Smith (United States)	....
Under 68 kilograms **Lightweight**	A. Fadzaev (EUN)	....
Under 74 kilograms **Welterweight**	J. Park (S. Korea)	....
Under 82 kilograms **Middleweight**	K. Jackson (United States)	....
Under 90 kilograms **Light heavyweight**	M. Khadartsev (EUN)	....
Under 100 kilograms **Heavyweight**	L. Khabelov (EUN)	....
Under 130 kilograms **Super heavyweight**	B. Baumgartner (United States)	....

VENUE: GEORGIA WORLD CONGRESS CENTER, OLYMPIC CENTER

Greco-Roman

Division	1992 winner	1996 winner
Under 48 kilograms **Light flyweight**	O. Koutcherenko (EUN)	....
Under 52 kilograms **Flyweight**	J. Ronningen (Norway)	....
Under 57 kilograms **Bantamweight**	H-B. An (S. Korea)	....
Under 62 kilograms **Featherweight**	M. Akif Pirim (Turkey)	....
Under 68 kilograms **Lightweight**	A. Repka (Hungary)	....
Under 74 kilograms **Welterweight**	M. Iskandarian (EUN)	....
Under 82 kilograms **Middleweight**	P. Farkas (Hungary)	....
Under 90 kilograms **Light heavyweight**	M. Bullman (Germany)	....
Under 100 kilograms **Heavyweight**	H. Milian (Cuba)	....
Under 130 kilograms **Super heavyweight**	A. Kareline (EUN)	....

DID YOU KNOW?

• Great Britain only competes in Freestyle wrestling at the Games.

John Smith (United States) and Kim Gwang Choi (N. Korea) get to grips in the featherweight event – Olympics 1992